SCIENCE 807
Machines 1

LIFEPAC Test is located in the center of the booklet. Please remove before starting the unit.

Authors:
Shirley A. Johnson, M.N.S.
Lee H. Dunning, M.S.T., M.S.Ed.

Editor:
Richard W. Wheeler, M.A.Ed.
Consulting Editor:
Harold Wengert, Ed.D.
Revision Editor:
Alan Christopherson, M.S.

Westover Studios Design Team:
Phillip Pettet, Creative Lead
Teresa Davis, DTP Lead
Nick Castro
Andi Graham
Jerry Wingo
Don Lechner

Alpha Omega
PUBLICATIONS

804 N. 2nd Ave. E.
Rock Rapids, IA 51246-1759

Machines 1

Introduction

All of the people in the world have had to work for a living since Adam and Eve were expelled from the garden of Eden (Genesis 3). In this LIFEPAC® you will learn about work as a scientist views it and about distance, force, and friction.

Do you work? Whenever you pick something up or move it against friction you perform work.

Objectives

Read these objectives. The objectives tell you what you will be able to do when you have successfully completed this LIFEPAC. When you have finished this LIFEPAC, you should be able to:

1. Measure distances in the metric and English systems.

2. Measure distances indirectly.

3. Define force.

4. Construct force diagrams.

5. Solve problems involving forces.

6. Explain and to apply Newton's Laws of motion.

7. Define work and energy.

8. Solve problems involving work and power.

Survey the LIFEPAC. Ask yourself some questions about this study and write your questions here.

_____
_____
_____
_____
_____
_____
_____
_____
_____
_____
_____
_____
_____
_____
_____
_____
_____
_____

1. DISTANCE

When you were small, distances were limited to your house and your yard. As you got older, your activities covered greater areas and your range increased to include church, school, homes of friends, and the streets joining those places.

Distance has varied meanings to people of different times and places. Society has therefore developed systems of measurement. Specific dimensions enable everyone to understand what is meant regardless of who is measuring or what is being measured.

SECTION OBJECTIVES

Review these objectives. When you have completed this section, you should be able to:

1.   Measure distances in the metric and English systems.
2.   Measure distances indirectly.

VOCABULARY

Study these words to enhance your learning success in this section.

cubit (kyü´bit). An ancient measure of length equal to 18 or 22 inches.

English system (Ing´glish sis´tum). The system of measurement that includes units like foot, pound, and gallon.

metric system (met´rik sis´tum). A system of measurement based on the meter as a unit of length.

Note: *All vocabulary words in this LIFEPAC appear in* **boldface** *print the first time they are used. If you are not sure of the meaning when you are reading, study the definitions given.*

Pronunciation Key: hat, āge, cãre, fär; let, ēqual, tėrm; it, īce; hot, ōpen, ôrder; oil; out; cup, pút, rüle; child; long; thin; /ŦH/ for then; /zh/ for measure; /u/ or /ə/ represents /a/ in about, /e/ in taken, /i/ in pencil, /o/ in lemon, and /u/ in circus.

DESCRIBING DISTANCE

Have you given someone directions to get to your house from school? What words did you use to describe the distance between the two places? In this section you will study ways to express distance.

Comparison. Many societies have no words to compare. One word may be used for *building* with no way to tell if the building is a tool shed or a skyscraper. Sometimes words, such as *far* or *near, large* or *small, high* or *low,* are as good as, or better than, exact measurement. Comparative words such as these can be used accurately in descriptions. People who use comparative words in conversation need more exact terms at other times.

With numbers. Over a period of several thousand years, people developed systems of measurement of distance. In Genesis 6 God commanded Noah to build an ark that was to be 300 **cubits** long, 50 cubits wide, and 30 cubits high. A cubit was the length of a forearm—from 46 to 56 centimeters (18 to 22 inches) long. The cubit, however, varied with the length of the arm. Another measurement from that portion of history was a *step* or a *pace.* The word *mile* comes from the Latin term for a thousand paces.

In the United States the common units used to measure distance are the *inch, foot, yard, and mile.* The problem with this system is the conversion from one unit to another. We have all learned that 5,280 feet equals a mile. A mile therefore is 63,360 inches, or 1,760 yards. Converting dimensions from feet to inches or from miles to feet requires clumsy multiplication or division. Engineers have used decimals to express fractions; but few others use decimals to express parts of feet, inches, or miles in the **English system**.

The history of the English system of units indicates that its origins are varied. At one time *inch* was the length of three dried barley corns laid end to end. At another time the inch was the width of a man's thumb. The *yard* was defined in 1120 AD by King Henry I of England as the distance from the end of his thumb to the tip of his nose when his arm was level.

France adopted the **metric system** in 1793. It was an entirely new system of measurement. The metric system is exact and easy to use because it is based on the decimal system, or multiples of ten. The metric system is used by scientists all over the world. In 1866 Congress legalized the use of the metric system in the United States. The Congress passed the Metric Conversion Act in 1975. However, each of these acts called for voluntary changeover and so very few Americans have learned the metric system. Therefore, the metric system is unfamiliar to most people in the United States. Using this system will require practice. Learning the metric system is like learning rules for a new game. The metric system will be used in most cases in this LIFEPAC.

The modern metric system is known as the International System of Units. The name International System of Units with the international abbreviation SI was given to the system by the General Conference on Weights and Measures in 1960.

In the SI system (from the French, *Systeme International d'Unites*) the fundamental unit of distance is the meter. For comparison, a meter is a little longer than a yard. A meter is divided into 100 units called *centimeters* and into 1,000 units called *millimeters.* The width of a large wire paper clip is about a centimeter and the diameter of the wire is about a millimeter. For long distances the convenient unit is the *kilometer,* 1,000 meters.

Match these items.

1.1	_____	Jeff's house is near school.	a.	comparative
1.2	_____	Sheri is nearly home.	b.	numerical
1.3	_____	Uncle Bob drives twenty miles to work.	c.	neither
1.4	_____	Jan is closer than Debbie to the goal.		
1.5	_____	February is shorter than June.		
1.6	_____	Dr. Davis is taller than Dr. Brown.		
1.7	_____	Dr. Davis is over six feet tall.		

Try this investigation to build your own cubit.

These supplies are needed:

- 10 strips of paper about 5 cm wide and at least 62 cm long
- scissors
- tape
- string

Follow these directions and answer the questions. Put a check in the box when each step is completed.

☐ 1. Ask each of ten students to place his forearm with fingers outstretched on a strip of paper. Mark the position of the elbow and the tip of the middle finger on each strip.

☐ 2. Trim the excess paper from the ends of each strip.

☐ 3. Organize the strips parallel to each other in order of length and tape one end of each along the edge of a table.

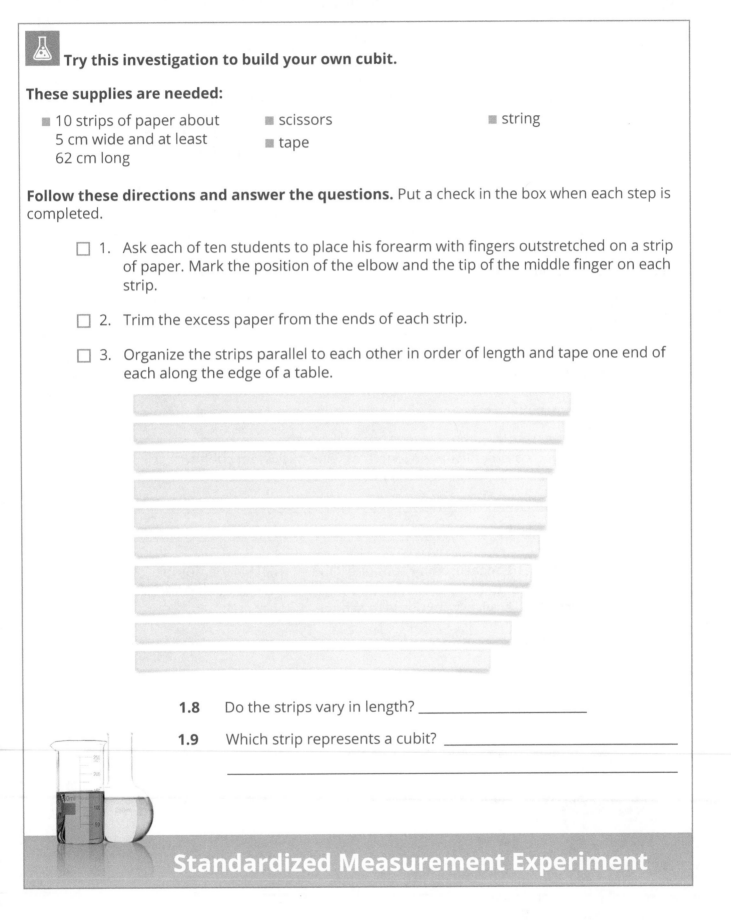

1.8 Do the strips vary in length? _____

1.9 Which strip represents a cubit? _____

_____

Standardized Measurement Experiment

☐ 4. Along some straight line (the wall, a floor board, an aisle) lay off twelve longest "cubits." Mark the starting point and the end.

☐ 5. From the same starting point lay off twelve shortest "cubits."

1.10 Using a shortest cubit as a unit of length (the same way you would use a ruler), what is the difference between twelve longest cubits and twelve shortest cubits?

_____

_____

☐ 6. Substitute a length of string for a strip of paper and remeasure a forearm.

1.11 What disadvantage is obvious in the use of string?

_____

_____

1.12 What common procedure could be used to make your classroom cubit more acceptable as a standard unit of length?

_____

_____

1.13 How could you communicate the length of your classroom cubit to a science class in another school?

_____

_____

Some things can be measured by counting. One example is the number of students in your class. Other things are measured using numbers but do not require counting; for instance, the distance from home to school.

Standardized Measurement Experiment

Write *count* before each quantity that is measured by counting.

1.14 _____ number of teachers in your school

1.15 _____ yesterday's high temperature

1.16 _____ length of the hall

1.17 _____ number of coins in a coin collection

1.18 _____ value of a coin in the collection

1.19 _____ number of centimeters in your height

1.20 _____ number of milliliters of water in a glass

1.21 _____ number of fans in a stadium

Answer these questions.

1.22 How could you find out, without counting, if more desks or more students were in a room?

_____

_____

1.23 How could you find out, without measuring, which of two cows gave more milk?

_____

_____

1.24 Without using numbers, how could you tell a store clerk the length of shoelace you need for your left sneaker?

_____

_____

1.25 Without using a ruler, which line is longer, or are the lines the same length?

_____

A   B

1.26 How did you discover the answer to 1.25?

_____

_____

 **Measure the following objects with a pac.**

1 pac = the width of the front cover of this LIFEPAC.

1.27 Measure the longer dimension of your desk top in pacs. _____

1.28 Measure the shorter dimension of your desk top in pacs. _____

1.29 Measure the length of your classroom in pacs. _____

1.30 Measure the width of your pen or pencil in pacs. _____

TEACHER CHECK _____ _____
                                    initials   date

Answer these questions.

1.31 What disadvantages are built into the pac as a standard unit of length?

_____

_____

1.32 How could you use the front cover of this LIFEPAC to measure the width of your pen or pencil? _____

_____

_____

1.33 What clue does activity 1.32 give to the development of the English system?

_____

_____

Multiply or divide to make these English distance conversions. Time yourself as you do the ten exercises without a calculator.

1 mile	= 5,280 feet

1.34   174 inches   = _____ feet

1.35   7 feet   = _____ inches

1.36   29 feet   = _____ yards

1.37   29 feet   = _____ inches

1.38   3 miles   = _____ feet

1.39   10,000 feet = _____ miles

1.40   10,000 feet = _____ yards

1.41   10,000 feet = _____ inches

1.42   79 yards   = _____ feet

1.43   100 yards   = _____ feet

Answer these questions.

1.44   How long did you take to work 1.34-1.43? _____

1.45   Which of the conversions were easier or faster than the rest?

      _____

      _____

1.46   Why were the conversions easier?

      _____

      _____

Multiply or divide to make these metric distance conversions. Time yourself as you do the ten exercises without a calculator.

> 1 kilometer = 1,000 meters
>
> 1 meter = 100 centimeters or 1,000 millimeters

1.47 174 centimeters = _____ meters

1.48 7 meters = _____ centimeters

1.49 29 centimeters = _____ millimeters

1.50 29 centimeters = _____ meters

1.51 3 kilometers = _____ meters

1.52 10,000 meters = _____ kilometers

1.53 10,000 meters = _____ centimeters

1.54 10,000 meters = _____ millimeters

1.55 79 millimeters = _____ centimeters

1.56 1,000 meters = _____ kilometers

Answer these questions.

1.57 How long did you take to work 1.47-1.56? _____

1.58 Explain the difference in your times.

_____

_____

Research and report.

1.59 Use outside sources to research one of these topics.

Isaac Newton   Robert Boyle

Nicolaus Copernicus   history of metric or English system

The report should be at least five handwritten, double-spaced pages including a short bibliography. Especially include a section on their Christian testimony.

TEACHER CHECK _____ _____
                                        initials   date

MEASURING DISTANCE

This section will cover direct and indirect measurement. You will learn to use a scale drawing to find unmeasurable distances.

Estimation. Between comparative words such as *large* and *small* and precise measurement lies the estimate. An estimate is a rough calculation or an educated guess.

Estimates are influenced by the surroundings. Many people underestimate distances indoors and overestimate them outdoors. Distances seem different over smooth and rough ground.

Distances are sometimes estimated by pacing. A pace is about 75 centimeters (30 inches). Estimating is visually or mentally comparing a distance to one that is known. An example of estimation is using the floor tiles to estimate the size of a room.

Estimation is sometimes used in science. Science, however, usually requires an exact statement of distance and other dimensions.

Direct measurement. Measurement with a meter stick is an example of direct measurement. It is the method preferred by scientists. Direct measurement using the metric system is used in track and field competition.

Short distances can be measured with a ruler or a tape. Laboratories try to use direct measurement for experiments. Accurate devices, such as *micrometers* and *vernier calipers,* have been developed for small distances. In the home the meter stick, yard stick, and tape measure are used. Surveyors use accurate steel tape measures for measuring distances for roads, canals, bridges, and boundaries.

Indirect measurement. Long ago the Greeks developed a form of mathematics called *geometry*. The word means *earth measure*. Euclid wrote a book 300 years before Christ that contained most of the mathematics of his time. This book, *Elements*, was a basic mathematics book for 2,000 years and was the beginning of geometry. It was translated into English in 1570.

Geometry is used by surveyors and mapmakers to represent distances that cannot be measured directly. A map is a *scale drawing* of an area of the earth's surface. In order to represent many miles of distance on the earth, the mapmaker uses lines on a paper that are shorter and *in proportion* to the actual distances. For example, a distance of 1 mile might be represented on a map by 1 inch. At that scale, 5 miles would equal 5 inches, 7.4 miles would equal 7.4 inches, and so on.

Complete these activities.

1.60 Write the *actual* distances represented by the following scale distances if the scale is 1 centimeter = 1 kilometer.

 a. 23 centimeters = _____ kilometers

 b. 1.6 centimeters = _____ kilometers

 c. 0.5 centimeters = _____ kilometers

 d. ¾ centimeters   = _____ kilometers

 e. 1³/₅ centimeters = _____ kilometers

 f. 9 centimeters   = _____ kilometers

1.61 Write the *scale* distances that represent the following actual distances if the scale is 1 inch = 1,000 feet.

 a. 4,000 feet   = _____ inches

 b. 10,000 feet   = _____ inches

 c. 21,000 feet   = _____ inches

 d. 900 feet   = _____ inches

 e. 1,500 feet   = _____ inches

 f. 40 feet   = _____ inch

1.62 Write the *actual* distances represented by the following scale distances if the scale is 1 centimeter = 5 kilometers.

 a. 2 centimeters   = _____ kilometers

 b. 5 centimeters   = _____ kilometers

 c. 10 centimeters = _____ kilometers

 d. 4.5 centimeters = _____ kilometers

 e. 0.8 centimeters = _____ kilometers

 f. 0.1 centimeters = _____ kilometer

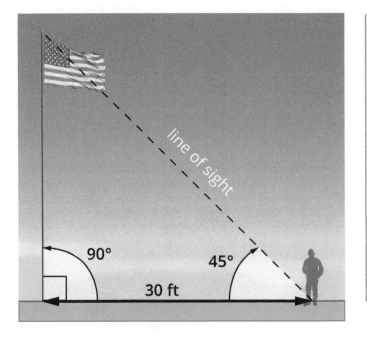

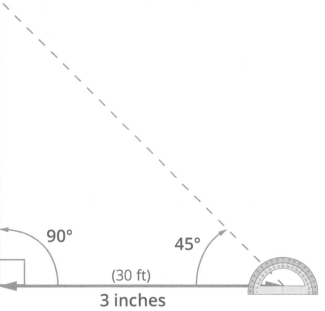

When an actual distance cannot be measured directly, a scale drawing can be set up that uses angles. For example, climbing a flagpole to measure its height is inconvenient at best. If, on the other hand, you measure the angle that the *line of sight* to the top of the pole makes with the ground, a scale drawing can be used to measure the height. We can say that, at a distance of 30 feet from the pole, the line of sight to the top makes an angle of 45° with the ground.

To construct a scale drawing, use a draftsman's triangle or the corner of a sheet of paper to draw the pole and the ground. Next, set up some convenient scale; say, 1 inch = 10 feet. Mark 3 inches (30 feet) from the base of the flagpole, and use a protractor to construct a 45° angle.

When the scale drawing is complete, measure the length of the line that represents the pole. You find that it is 3 inches long. At a scale of 1 inch = 10 feet, the pole must be 30 feet tall.

✏️ **Answer these questions.**

1.63 How many degrees are contained in the angle at a corner of this page? _____

1.64 How could you construct a 45° angle if you had neither a draftsman's triangle nor a protractor?

_____

_____

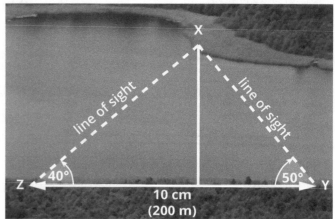

Example 1. Find the height of a tree. An observer notes that at 25 meters from the base, the line of sight to the top of the tree makes an angle of 45° (half a right angle) with the ground.

The observer makes a scale drawing with a scale of 1 cm = 5 m. The base line is 5 cm long with a 45° angle at one end, and the line of sight is drawn to form a triangle. If the tree is 5 cm on the scale drawing, the tree is actually 25 meters high.

Example 2. From two points on Lakeshore Drive (Z and Y) a boulder (X) is sighted across the lake. The sketch is a scale drawing. What is the shortest distance between the boulder and the highway?

The base line representing 200 meters is 10 centimeters (1 cm = 20 m). The angles are laid out with the use of a protractor. The vertex of the triangle represents the boulder. The line on the sketch representing the shortest distance across the lake is 4.9 centimeters. The actual distance across the lake is therefore 98 meters.

This same idea of indirect measurement is used to measure the distance to the closer stars. A very long base line is needed so astronomers use the diameter of the earth's orbit. They measure the angle to a star and six months later measure it again. From these measurements, the star/earth distance can be determined.

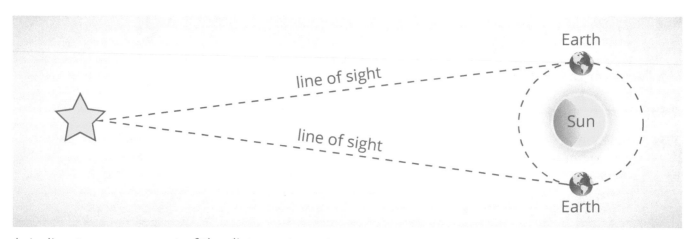

| Indirect measurement of the distance to a star

Complete these activities.

A line of sight to the top of a tree meets the ground 20 meters from the trunk at an angle of 45°.

1.65 How tall is the tree?

_____

1.66 If you do not have a protractor or a draftsman's triangle, how could you construct a 45° angle?

_____

_____

_____

_____

1.67 How could you construct a 22¾° angle? _____

_____

_____

1.68 Two straight roads intersect at one end of a lake. The roads form an angle of 30° with each other. The widest part of the lake is 1,000 m from the intersection along one road and 1,200 m from the intersection along the other road. Make a new scale drawing similar to the sample of this problem.

How wide is the lake?

_____

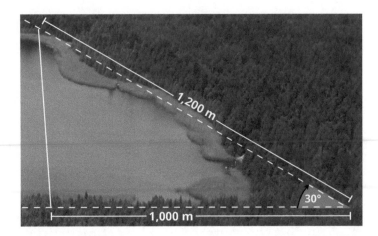

1.69 A flagpole casts a shadow 10 m long. An imaginary line from the end of the shadow to the top of the pole forms an angle of 67½° with the ground.

How tall is the flagpole?

_____

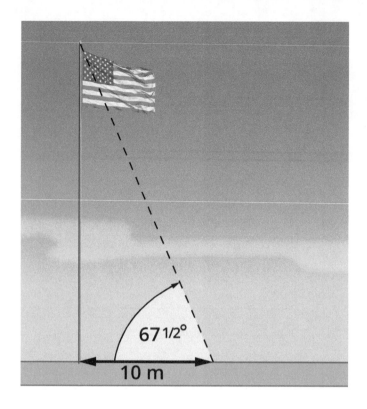

Review the material in this section in preparation for the Self Test. The Self Test will check your mastery of this particular section. The items missed on this Self Test will indicate specific areas where restudy is needed for mastery.

SELF TEST 1

Write the letter of the correct choice (each answer, 2 points).

1.01 The cubit was known as early as _____ .
  a. 1750   b. 1400   c. AD 1   d. 2500 BC

1.02 The metric system was devised by _____ .
  a. Sophocles   b. Moses   c. the Romans   d. the French

1.03 The system of measurements that includes the foot, yard, and mile is the _____ system.
  a. English   b. French   c. metric   d. electric

1.04 A mile contains _____ feet.
  a. 63,360   b. 5,280   c. 1,492   d. 1,000

1.05 In the United States the metric system is most commonly used by _____ .
  a. auto mechanics   b. grocers   c. scientists   d. bus drivers

Make these conversions (each answer, 3 points).

1.06 10 cm   = _____ mm

1.07 100 cm   = _____ m

1.08 25 m   = _____ cm

1.09 73 m   = _____ mm

1.010 147 mm = _____ m

Calculate the distances (each answer, 5 points).

1.011 Use the scale drawing to find the actual distance AB.

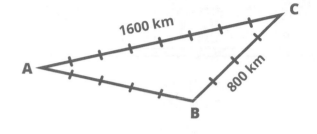

1.012 Use a scale drawing to find the height of a tree if it casts a shadow 30 m and the line from the top of the tree to the top of the shadow forms an angle of 45° with the ground.

Complete these sentences (each answer, 3 points).

1.013 Measuring the distance to a planet would probably require the use of _____ (direct / indirect) measurement.

1.014 The system of mathematics used for, among other things, surveying and indirect measurements is _____ .

1.015 The term that means 1,000 meters is _____ .

1.016 The metric system is based on multiples of the number _____ .

1.017 The fundamental unit of length in the metric system is the _____ .

1.018 An educated guess of a distance is a(n) _____ .

42 / 53

SCORE _____   TEACHER _____ _____

initials   date

2. FORCE

All around us are forces of nature. Some of them we understand. Others remain mysteries. In Job 37:5 we read that God does "great things...which we cannot comprehend." Over many years God has revealed to mankind what we know about **force**.

Two giants of science, Galileo and Newton, investigated forces in general and the force of gravity in particular. Forces and their effects conform to patterns of behavior called laws of motion. These laws are absolute and hold true in the whole universe. This fact illustrates that God created the universe and it operates in an orderly, precise manner according to His laws. This fact is opposite to the theories of evolution where chance controls our universe.

SECTION OBJECTIVES

Review these objectives. When you have completed this section, you should be able to:

3.   Define force.

4.   Construct force diagrams.

5.   Solve problems involving forces.

6.   Explain and to apply Newton's laws of motion.

VOCABULARY

Study these words to enhance your learning success in this section.

accelerate (ak sel´u rāt). Change of velocity.

diagonal (dī ag´u nul). A straight line from corner to corner in a parallelogram.

force (fôrs). A push or a pull.

gravity (grav´u tē). The force that objects exert on each other because of their mass.

inertia (in er shu). The property of matter that resists change in velocity.

magnitude (mag´nu tüd). Size.

newton (nü´tun). The unit of force in the metric system.

proportion (pru pôr´shun). Relation in size of one thing to another.

scalar (skā´lur). A quantity that has size only.

velocity (vu los´u tē). Speed in a given direction.

THE MEANING OF FORCE

A **force** is a push or a pull. In physical science force is a vector quantity. Vector quantities have both **magnitude** and direction. A force cannot be seen, but the results of a force may be seen. You can see a baseball move from the pitcher's hand to the bat. The force of the bat causes the ball to change direction and move back toward the pitcher. A ball thrown into the air reaches a peak and returns to earth.

Gravity. An ever-present example of force is **gravity**. Gravity is the force of the earth on objects near it. The first recorded scientific observations of gravity were made by Galileo. He related the distance a metal ball rolls down a slanted board to the time it required. He also demonstrated that heavy objects and light objects fall at the same rate.

Galileo's hypothesis was tested but he could not measure either speed or time accurately with the instruments available.

Measurement. In the metric system a force is measured in **newtons** (N). Newtons can be measured in terms of mass, distance, and time. One newton is equal to 0.22 pounds or one pound equals 4.45 newtons. Instead of measuring an object rolling down a slanted board as Galileo did, we can study an object in free fall. The force causing it to fall is the attraction of earth's gravity on the object.

Galileo. Galileo Galilei was an Italian who was born in Pisa in 1564. His father was interested in music and classical literature. Galileo was sent to the University of Pisa to study medicine. There, he invented a pendulum timer to take pulse rates. During his studies he became interested in the physical sciences and mathematics.

When he was twenty-six years old, he became professor of mathematics at Pisa. Because he disagreed with the established theories of his time, he made enemies of other professors. He left Pisa and went to Padua where he studied astronomy and, again, disagreed with the other professors. These studies conflicted with the established Roman Catholic Church views. The church held that the earth was the center of the universe. Galileo, on the other hand, taught that the sun was the center of our part of the universe and that the earth moved around the sun. He also wrote books that enraged other professors. He was tried for heresy by a church court. He was forced to confess that he taught ideas of which the church disapproved. Then Galileo was placed under house arrest. Galileo believed in God, but he wanted freedom to investigate.

Complete these sentences.

2.1   A push or a pull is a(n) _____ .

2.2   Quantities that must be defined by their size and direction are called _____ .

2.3   The force of attraction that the earth exerts on all objects is called _____ .

2.4   The metric unit of force is the _____ .

2.5   The most powerful social institution of Galileo's time was the _____ .

Write true or false.

2.6 _____ Galileo was limited by a lack of money.

2.7 _____ Galileo's discoveries were based almost exclusively on guesswork.

2.8 _____ Galileo believed that the planets revolved around the sun.

2.9 _____ Galileo's scientific views were accepted soon after they were published.

Try this investigation.

These supplies are needed:

- thin cardboards (8½" x 11")
- rubber bands
- paper clips
- 25 identical washers

Follow these directions. Put a check in the box when each step is completed.

☐ 1. Punch a small hole near the top center of a cardboard. Insert a section of one rubber band and loop a paper clip through the rubber band on the back of the cardboard to keep it from pulling out.

☐ 2. Unbend a paper clip to form a hook. Hang the clip from the rubber band on the front side of the cardboard.

☐ 3. Add washers to the hook until the rubber band begins to stretch. Number of washers _____ . These washers are to be considered part of the hook and should not be listed on the data table. If the rubber band does not need to be straightened, do not use any washers.

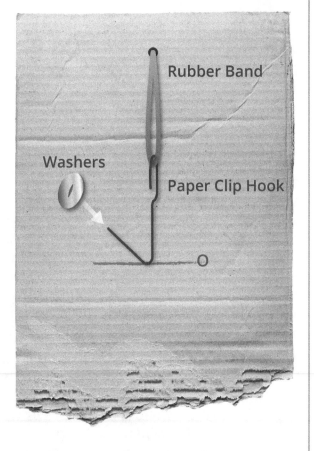

Force Measurement Experiment

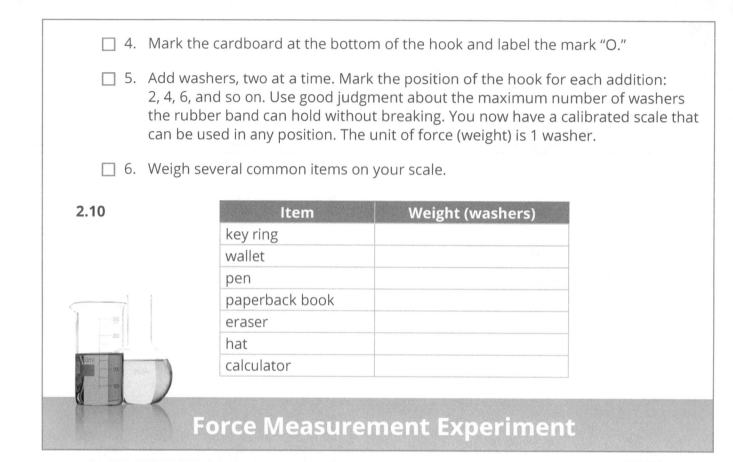

☐ 4. Mark the cardboard at the bottom of the hook and label the mark "O."

☐ 5. Add washers, two at a time. Mark the position of the hook for each addition: 2, 4, 6, and so on. Use good judgment about the maximum number of washers the rubber band can hold without breaking. You now have a calibrated scale that can be used in any position. The unit of force (weight) is 1 washer.

☐ 6. Weigh several common items on your scale.

2.10

Item	Weight (washers)
key ring	
wallet	
pen	
paperback book	
eraser	
hat	
calculator	

Force Measurement Experiment

THE LAWS OF NEWTON

Before Newton's time, other scientists had been aware of an attraction the earth has for all objects near it. Galileo, for one, had experimented; but he was limited by the lack of appropriate measuring devices. Newton's genius led him to state physical relationships that he had never observed operating and to invent a system of mathematics (calculus) that enabled him to explain them.

Sir Isaac Newton. Isaac Newton was born on Christmas Day in 1642. He was a poor farm boy in Woolsthorpe, Lincolnshire, England. Reading, invention, and mathematics were his favorite pastimes. An uncle enabled him to attend Trinity College of Cambridge University when he was eighteen. He graduated in 1665 with no significant list of achievements.

The young student spent much time thinking. He noticed that as an apple fell from the tree it always fell straight toward the center of the earth. Newton explained this observation in terms of the pull that exists between the earth and all other objects. This pull is called the *force of gravity*.

Gravity cannot be explained; it is a pull that exists between all objects, however large or small. The best that scientists can do is to say that it exists and to express it mathematically. Gravity, electrostatic force, and magnetic force hold the universe together. The writer to the Hebrews (Hebrews 1:3) explains this type of force as the essence of Christ's power.

Among Newton's other mathematical and scientific discoveries were his three laws of motion:

1. An object that is moving will continue to move at the same speed in a straight line, and an object standing still will continue to stand still, *unless* a push or pull (a force) causes a change.

2. If a force does cause a change in an object's speed, the change in speed will be large if the force is large or small if the force is small. The change in speed will be large for small objects (small mass) and small for large objects (large mass). A small car is easier to push than is a large car. The same engine (the same push) in a small car and in a large car would give the small car a greater **acceleration**. If the force causes the object to speed up, you have acceleration; if the force causes the object to slow down, you have deceleration.

3. Forces never occur singly. Each force (action) is accompanied by another force (reaction) that is the same size, but is opposite in direction. For example, when you push on a door, the door pushes back on you.

Newton returned to Cambridge to be named professor of mathematics. He wrote books and presented many papers to the Royal Society.

About 1692 Newton had a nervous breakdown, which ended his new discoveries. In 1699 Newton was named master of the mint. He almost completely stopped counterfeiting in England. He also served in Parliament representing Cambridge University.

Sir Isaac Newton died in 1727.

First law of motion. When you are riding in a car that stops suddenly, you continue to move forward. If the car is standing still and suddenly starts, your body is pushed back into the seat.

The first experience is an example of an object (your body) remaining in motion in a straight line unless a force (the car's brakes acting through your seat belt) acts on it. The second experience is an example of an object (your body) at rest remaining at rest unless a force (the car seat back) acts on it.

This tendency of mass to resist change is **inertia**. Experiments have shown that the mass and inertia of a body are **proportional**. The greater the mass, the greater the inertia; the smaller the mass, the smaller the inertia.

When the car in which you are riding stops suddenly, your body (unless you have on your seat belt) wishes to continue moving straight ahead. When the stopped car starts, your body wants to stay where it is and pushes against the seat when the car's seat moves forward. The faster an object is moving the greater is its resistance to stopping.

The effect of inertia on the spinning earth is the bulge at the equator. The earth's surface wants to continue in a straight line, but it is pulled into a circular path by the cohesion of the rock beneath.

Second law of motion. The second law of motion explains how force, acceleration, and mass are related. As the mass increases, the force needed to accelerate it must increase also. In the metric system, force is in newtons and mass is in kilograms.

Third law of motion. A book on a desk exerts a downward force on the desk. The desk pushes up on the book with an equal force. When a swimmer dives off a raft, his push on the raft results in the movement of the raft. The equal push that the raft exerts on the swimmer causes him to be propelled forward into the water.

The statement that every action is accompanied by an equal and opposite reaction explains the "kick" of a gun. The force of the bullet leaving the gun is equal to the force the bullet gives the gun in the opposite direction.

✏️ **Complete this activity.**

Write Newton's laws of motion in your own words.

2.11 first law: _____

_____

_____

_____

_____

2.12 second law: _____

_____

_____

_____

_____

2.13 third law: _____

_____

_____

_____

_____

SCIENCE 807

LIFEPAC TEST

NAME _____

DATE _____

SCORE _____

51 / 64

SCIENCE 807: LIFEPAC TEST

Match these items (each answer, 2 points). Answers may be used more than once.

1. _____ force   a. second
2. _____ distance   b. watt
3. _____ work   c. ampere
4. _____ power   d. newton
5. _____ energy   e. meter
6. _____ time   f. joule
7. _____ weight   g. kilogram
                                h. degree

Write true or false (each answer, 1 point).

8. _____ Energy is the ability to do work.

9. _____ Vector P is equal to vector Q.

10. _____ A quantity that has direction as well as size is a scalar.

11. _____ A force is a push or a pull.

12. _____ The potential energy of an object is equal to the work required to lift it into position.

Complete these sentences (each answer, 3 points).

13. The man who formulated statements that describe the relationships between forces and motion was _____ .

14. The man who originally wrote about observations of gravity was _____ .

15. A quantity that has both size and direction is a(n) _____ .

16. A skater gliding on ice is an example of the _____ law of motion.

17. A car starting to move is an example of the _____ law of motion.

18. A balloon blown up and then released is an example of the _____ law of motion.

19. Two cars colliding is an example of the _____ law of motion.

20. A key ring swung on a chain is an example of the _____ law of motion.

21. Energy possessed by a moving object is _____ energy.

22. The rate at which work is done is called _____ .

Complete these items (each answer, 5 points).

23. Use the scale drawing to find the distance represented by AB.

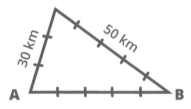

24. Construct the vector sum of the two vectors.

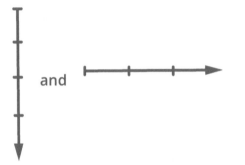

and

25. Calculate the power developed by a motor that moves an object 8 m against a force of 10 N in 4 sec.

⚗ Complete this activity.

2.14 Use your calibrated force scale to measure the force required to pull a hardcover book across a table at a constant slow speed.

Put the book on sleds of slick cardboard, aluminum foil, cloth, and four other substances of your devising. For each surface measure the force required to move the book across the table at the same constant, slow speed. If necessary to keep the book from moving around on the sled, tuck part of the sled between pages of the book. Pull parallel to the desk top.

Answer these questions.

2.15 Which surface produced the greatest frictional force?

_____

2.16 Which surface produced the smallest frictional force?

_____

2.17 Choose any one surface. Watch your scale carefully as you begin to pull the book at a constant, slow speed. What is true of the force required to *start* the book moving, compared to the force required to keep it moving?

_____

2.18 Watch your scale carefully as you begin to pull the book to a significantly higher speed. What is true of the force required to attain the higher speed?

_____

Item	Force (washers)
Hardcover book	
- on cardboard	
- on foil	
- on cloth	

Force of Friction Experiment

FORCE VECTORS

A force is described by its size and direction. This size of force is measured in newtons. A gentle pull is a small force. A shove is a large force. A force has both size and direction. The direction of the pull in a tug of war is obvious, as is the direction of a racket on a tennis ball. Forces may be represented in a diagram by arrows.

The head of the arrow points in the direction of the force. The magnitude of the force is indicated by the length of the arrow.

Vector quantities. Any quantity that has both size (magnitude) and direction is called a vector quantity. If a quantity has magnitude only, it is a **scalar** quantity. An example of a scalar quantity is mass, which has no direction. Another example of a scalar quantity is speed. **Velocity** is a vector quantity made up of a scalar quantity (speed) and a direction.

Vector diagrams. Suppose you want to show the magnitude and direction of a quantity. The vector arrow is a meaningful diagram if you know the scale. Imagine a force of 10 newtons in a westward direction. Let 1 centimeter represent 2 newtons. The diagram would look like this:

5 cm west

A force of 20 newtons north using a scale of 1 centimeter for 10 newtons, is represented in this way:

2 cm north

A velocity of 80 kilometers per hour to the east (10 kilometers equals 1 centimeter) is represented in this way:

8 cm east

Sometimes a direction is given in degrees. An example is a force of ten newtons pulling at 45°. With a scale of 1 centimeter representing five newtons the vector would look like this:

2 cm @ 45°

Vector addition and subtraction. Forces can be added. A car is pushed with a force of 10 newtons to the west. Then a second force of 10 newtons to the west is added. The car is being pushed with a total force (the *resultant* force) of 20 N west. If 2 cm represents 10 N, the force diagram would look like this:

10N
10N
2 cm west

Conventionally, the two 10 N-forces are represented by a single force vector:

20N
4 cm west

In a tug of war, five boys pull east with a force of 20 N each. Four boys pull west with a force of 22 newtons each. Let 1 cm represent 25 N.

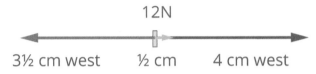

mud

88N   100N

3½ cm west   4 cm west

The vector difference (the resultant) is 12 N east.

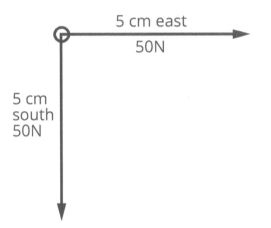

12N

3½ cm west   ½ cm   4 cm west

Now imagine two forces not acting in a straight line. When a wire fence is strung, the wire is tightened on each side of a corner post so that the force is 50 newtons on each side of the 90° angle. Using a scale of 1 centimeter to represent ten newtons, draw the two vectors.

5 cm east
50N

5 cm
south
50N

Now complete the rectangle. Draw the **diagonal** from the post to the opposite corner.

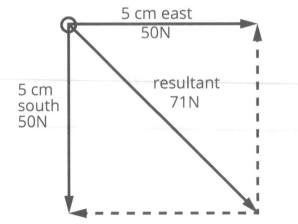

5 cm east
50N

5 cm
south
50N

resultant
71N

Measure the diagonal. It is 7.1 centimeters. If each centimeter represents 10 N, the magnitude of the resultant is 71 newtons. Use a protractor to measure the angle. It is 45°. The resultant, then, is 71 N at 45° with the fence.

The *resultant* is the *vector sum* of two or more vector quantities. In other words, if the single 71-N force, which is the resultant, acted on the fence post, the effect would be *the same* as if the two 50-N forces acted at right angles.

An alternate way of constructing a vector sum is to "walk out" the vectors one at a time. For example, taking the previous two vectors, "walk out" the first and then "walk out" the second, without lifting your pencil. This is the same as adding the vectors head-to-tail.

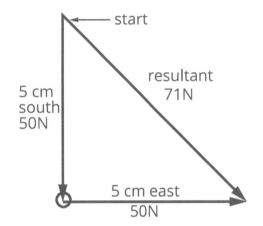

start

5 cm
south
50N

resultant
71N

5 cm east
50N

The resultant (the vector sum) again is a vector representing 71 N at 45° with the fence. Vectors can be moved, so long as they maintain their original length and direction.

If a vector is represented by 10 N, then -10 N is another vector of the same size pointing in the opposite direction.

10N   -10N

Write true or false.

2.19 _____ The vector ↘ is the same as the vector ↘ .

2.20 _____ The vector ↗ is the negative of ↙ .

2.21 _____ A vector may be moved without changing its meaning.

2.22 _____ Constructing a rectangle is the only way to find a vector sum.

2.23 _____ A vector sum is always equal to the sum of the magnitudes of the vectors being added.

Complete these activities.

Vectors are often represented with right-pointing arrows above their names as seen in the drawings below.

2.24 Construct the vector sum of vectors $\vec{A}$ and $\vec{B}$.

2.25 Construct the resultant of vectors $\vec{M}$ and $\vec{N}$.

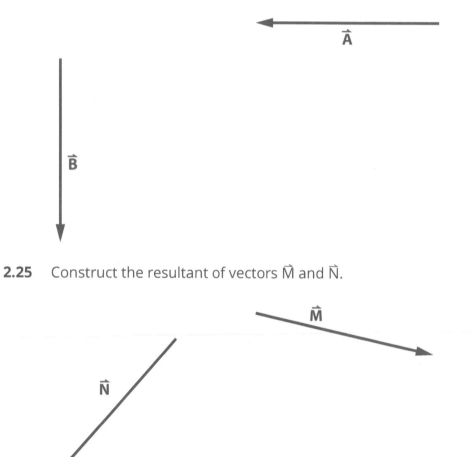

2.26   Sketch the negative of $\vec{P}$.

Review the material in this section in preparation for the Self Test. This Self Test will check your mastery of this particular section as well as your knowledge of the previous section.

SELF TEST 2

Match these items (each answer, 2 points).

2.01	_____ a small car is easier to push than a large car	a. first law of motion
2.02	_____ a skater glides	b. second law of motion
2.03	_____ a rifle kicks	c. third law of motion
2.04	_____ a balloon gyrates	
2.05	_____ a car brakes	
2.06	_____ a book rests	
2.07	_____ a light ball travels farther than a heavy ball when kicked	
2.08	_____ two cars collide	
2.09	_____ a satellite orbits	
2.010	_____ a ball hit by a man travels faster than one hit by a boy	

Complete these statements (each answer, 3 points).

2.011 A quantity that has direction as well as size is a(n) _____ .

2.012 A push or a pull exerted on an object is a(n) _____ .

2.013 The force that attracts all objects toward the earth is _____ .

2.014 For two vector quantities to be equal, they have the same direction and the same _____ .

2.015 Galileo was a native of _____ .

2.016 Galileo taught that the _____ was not the center of the universe.

2.017 Newton was a native of _____ .

2.018 The system of measurement based on multiples of ten is the _____ system.

2.019 The meter is the basic unit of length in the _____ system.

2.020 The use of angles and scale drawings to determine actual distances is called _____ measurement.

Write true or false (each answer, 1 point).

2.021 _____ A equals – B   A ———→ B ←———

2.022 _____ Thirty furlongs per fortnight is a vector quantity.

2.023 _____ Gravity is called a force because it pulls objects to the earth.

2.024 _____ The church opposed Galileo's right to present his scientific findings.

2.025 _____ Subsequently, the church's views on astronomy were proved inaccurate.

2.026 _____ Galileo believed in God.

2.027 _____ Newton was the first to experiment with gravity.

Complete these activities (each answer, 5 points).

2.028 Construct the vector sum $\vec{M} + \vec{N}$.

$\vec{M}$ $\vec{N}$

Use ———→ to present the *magnitude* of one unit vector for 2.029 and 2.030.

2.029 Construct a vector three units long, pointing to the left.

• START

2.030 Construct a vector two units toward the lower right corner of this page.

START •

2.031 Find the vector sum of the two vectors.

2.032 Robin Hood wants to measure the length of a rope his merry men have recently detached from a deputy sheriff. Robin stands on a cliff and shoots an arrow, with the rope attached, at a hamburger on the plain below. Little John paces 30 yards from the foot of the cliff to the hamburger, and measures 45° between the taut cord and the ground.

 a. How long is the cord (this part, 4 points)?

 _____

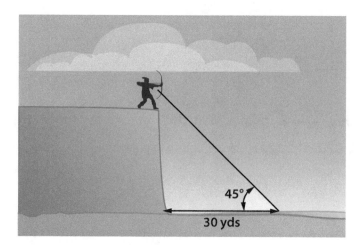

45°

30 yds

 b. This method is an example of _____ (direct, indirect) measurement (this part, 1 point).

66 / 82   SCORE _____   TEACHER _____ _____
initials   date

3. WORK

Perhaps when you get home from school you say, "I worked hard today." **Work** is often used as a synonym for something to do, an occupation. The Bible refers many times to work, toil, and labor in the sense of something to do. In Genesis 3:19 God commanded Adam to toil and sweat. In Matthew 11:28 Jesus says, "Come unto me, all ye that labor and are heavy laden, and I will give you rest."

In science, *work* has another meaning. You will study this scientific meaning in this section.

Make a chart of the formulas and unit definitions as you proceed through this section.

Examples:

- work = force x distance   w = f × d
- force = lbs. (English) or newtons (N) (metric)
- work = newton-meters (metric) or ft. lbs. (English)
- 1 joule (J) = 1 newton-meter (N-m)

SECTION OBJECTIVES

Review these objectives. When you have completed this section, you should be able to:

7.   Define work and energy.

8.   Solve problems involving work and power.

VOCABULARY

Study these words to enhance your learning success in this section.

energy (en′ ur jē). The ability to do work.

horsepower (hôrs′pou ur). English system unit of power, equivalent to 746 watts.

joule (joul). Metric unit of work, and energy, equal to one newton times one meter.

kinetic energy (ki net′ik en′ur jē). Energy of motion.

potential energy (pu ten′shul en′ur jē). Energy of position.

power (pou′ur). The rate of doing work.

watt (wot). Metric unit of power equal to one joule per second.

work (wė rk). The product of force and the distance through which it moves.

WORK DEFINED

As you sit reading this material, you might say you are working. Biologically, you are converting stored energy to heat. Physically, however, you are doing no work because no force is being exerted and no movement is taking place.

Definition. As understood by the physical scientist, work depends upon (1) the size of the force and (2) the distance through which the force moves.

- work = force × distance

If you push against a wall and the wall does not move, no work is done. If you lift a box, the work done depends on how high the box moves and on the force needed to lift it. The force must be in the same direction as the motion for work to be done.

Units. Distance is measured in meters and force in newtons. Work is measured in **joules** (newton-meters). One newton producing movement through a distance of one meter is called a joule.

The unit of work, the joule, was named for the English physicist, James Prescott Joule (1818-89). During the 1840's Joule did many experiments with energy and heat. He related energy produced by machines to units of heat. Joule used pounds, feet, and degrees Fahrenheit for his experiments because at that time England did not use the metric system.

Mathematics. Work is force that causes movement times the distance through which the force moves: $w = f \times d$. Force is a vector quantity, which can be shown by putting a little arrow over the f, like this: $\vec{f}$

- $w = \vec{f} \times d$

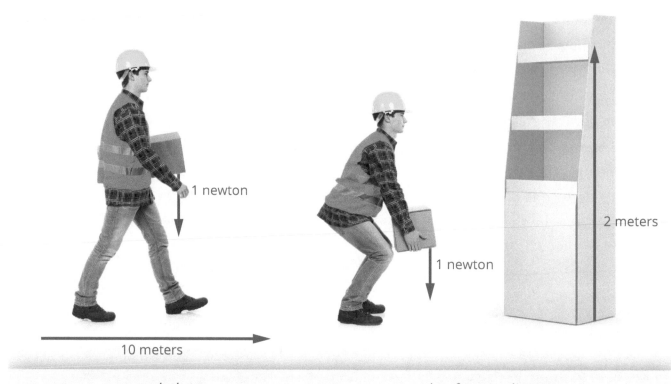

no work done

10 meters

1 newton

work = force x distance
= 1 newton x 2 meters
= 2 joules

1 newton

2 meters

In the metric system the unit of force is the newton (N) and the unit of work is the joule (J).

Work is not done unless motion is in the same direction as the force. If a package that weighs one newton is carried ten meters across a level floor, no work is done (except the little used to overcome air resistance) because the movement is horizontal and the force is vertical.

Work is done when force and motion are in the same direction. If a force of one newton is used to lift a box two meters, work is done.

Write true or false.

3.1 _____ Work is done if you push against the wall.

3.2 _____ Work is done if you push a box across the room.

3.3 _____ Work is done if water falls from the top of the dam.

3.4 _____ Work is done if you lift a brick.

3.5 _____ Work is done if you push a child in a wagon.

3.6 _____ Work is done if you carry a book across the room.

Complete these activities.

3.7 A box of groceries requires five newtons of force to lift it one meter to the counter. How much work is done?

3.8 A force of 10 newtons is used to lift a boy 3 meters into the air. How much work is done?

3.9 A man weighing 50 newtons climbs a 2-meter ladder. How much work is done?

3.10 How much work is done when a book weighing 2.00125 N is carried from a desk in one classroom to a desk in another, 25.796 m along a straight hall? Explain.

WORK AND ENERGY

You cannot see **energy**, but you can see what energy does. Energy has no mass. It does not occupy space. The physical definition of energy is the ability to do work. If work is the motion of an object through a distance, and energy can move an object, then energy and work are related.

Kinetic energy. **Kinetic energy** is the energy of motion. The amount of energy an object in motion possesses depends on (1) its speed and (2) its mass. A ball with a mass of 0.25 kilograms and a speed of 80 kilometers per hour has less kinetic energy than a ball with a mass of 1.0 kilograms moving with the same speed. Water rushing downhill has kinetic energy and a boy going down a ramp on a skateboard also has kinetic energy.

Potential energy. Stored energy is called **potential energy**. A marble resting on the edge of a table has potential energy. When it rolls over the edge, the potential energy becomes kinetic energy. The work done to give

an object potential energy is found by multiplying its weight (force of gravity) by the height to which it is raised.

Examples of stored energy are water stored behind a dam, a book resting on a table, and a child's wagon at the top of a hill.

Early in history people learned to use water for turning a wheel to grind wheat, to pump water, to cut logs, and to do many other basic activities of people. The kinetic energy of water falling or running down was changed to mechanical energy.

Today the falling water from dams is used to turn turbines that generate electricity. Thus, kinetic energy becomes electrical energy, which might become heat, light, or mechanical energy in homes and factories.

Energy is measured by the amount of work that it does. The potential energy of an object is the same as the work required to lift it into position.

Complete these activities.

3.11 A 500 lb. pile driver is raised to a height of 12 feet, then dropped. (The English unit for work is ft. lbs.)

    a. How much work is done on the pile driver in raising it?

    b. What is the increase in the pile driver's potential energy?

c. What is the *maximum* kinetic energy the pile driver will have after it is released?

3.12 A box weighing 4 N is lifted 3 m.

a. How much work is done on the box?

b. How much potential energy does the box possess at the top?

3.13 A trunk is dragged 3 m across an attic floor by a force of 2 N.

a. How much work is done on the trunk?

b. Assuming the floor to be level, what is the gain in potential energy?

c. What frictional force resisted the movement of the trunk?

WORK AND POWER

Two men stacking cement blocks will not work at the same rate. Work is the product of a force moving an object through a distance. If each man lifts a hundred 1-newton blocks to a height of 2 meters, each one does the same amount of work. If, however, one man is capable of doing his work faster than the other, the concept of **power** comes under consideration.

Power. Three factors determine the amount of power: force, distance, and time. The mathematical form is:

$$\text{power} = \frac{\text{work}}{\text{time}}$$

Power is the rate, or speed, of doing work.

The rate of doing work is important in many ways. For many activities that are properly called work, time is important. For instance, when a force of 100 newtons is used to lift an anvil to a work bench 1 meter high, how much work is done?

$$\text{work} = f \times d = 100 \text{ newtons} \times 1 \text{ meter}$$

$$= 100 \text{ joules}$$

Power is work divided by time. If four seconds is required to lift the anvil, how much power is developed?

$$\text{power} = \frac{\text{force} \times \text{distance}}{\text{time}} = \frac{\text{work}}{\text{time}}$$

$$\text{power} = \frac{100 \text{ N-m}}{4 \text{ sec.}} = \frac{100 \text{ joules}}{4 \text{ sec.}}$$

$$= \frac{25 \text{ joules}}{4 \text{ sec.}}$$

Units. When James Watt built steam engines in the 1760s, he needed a system upon which to base a rental fee. He compared the engines to strong workhorses that could lift 150 pounds at 3⅔ feet per second. Watt defined 550 foot pounds per second as one **horsepower**.

In the metric system power is expressed in **watts**, after James Watt. One watt of power is one joule of work performed in one second.

$$1 \text{ watt} = \frac{1 \text{ joules}}{1 \text{ sec.}}$$

The horsepower unit of the English system is 746 watts. Today the horsepower is still in common use. All engines and motors have horsepower ratings.

The power of a machine may be compared with the power of Jesus Christ to change a life. The love of God is all powerful and everlasting. His spiritual power is the greatest resource in our lives.

 Please complete the following activity.

3.14 An elevator weighing 2,000 lbs. is raised eleven stories in 20 seconds. If the distance between stories is 10 feet, how much power is developed by the elevator motor?
Remember: 550 ft.-lbs./sec. = 1 HP

🧪 **Try this investigation of "manpower."** Ask several members of your class to cooperate with you on this investigation.

These supplies are needed:

■ watch or stopwatch ■ scale to weigh students ■ tape measure or yardstick

Follow these directions and answer the questions. Put a check in the box when each step is completed.

☐ 1. Weigh each helper and record the data.

3.15

Helper	Weight (lbs.)	Rise (feet)	Time (seconds)	Power (ft.-lbs./sec.)	Horsepower
a.	b.	c.	d.	e.	f.

☐ 2. Select a staircase, steep hill, or other safe incline. Secure your teacher's approval on the appropriateness of the incline you have chosen.

TEACHER CHECK _____ _____
　　　　　　　　　　　　　initials　　　date

☐ 3. Measure the vertical distance between the bottom and top of the incline. If you cannot measure the vertical distance, try to apply the idea of indirect measurement from Section 1.

☐ 4. Use a stopwatch or sweep second hand to time each helper as he sprints up the incline.

☐ 5. Calculate the power generated by each helper, in ft.-lbs./sec. and in horsepower. Remember: 550 ft.-lbs./sec. = 1 HP

Power Experiment

3.16 In comparing two people of about the same physical condition, what is the relationship between the power generated by a heavy individual and that of a light one?

_____

_____

_____

3.17 In comparing two people of about the same weight, what is the relationship between the power generated by a well-conditioned individual and one who is not in condition?

_____

_____

_____

3.18 Could your helpers maintain their power output for an extended time?

_____

TEACHER CHECK _____ _____
                    initials   date

Power Experiment

Before you take this last Self Test, you may want to do one or more of these self checks.

1. _____ Read the objectives. See if you can do them.
2. _____ Restudy the material related to any objectives that you cannot do.
3. _____ Use the **SQ3R** study procedure to review the material:
   a. **S**can the sections.
   b. **Q**uestion yourself.
   c. **R**ead to answer your questions.
   d. **R**ecite the answers to yourself.
   e. **R**eview areas you did not understand.
4. _____ Review all vocabulary, activities, and Self Tests, writing a correct answer for every wrong answer.

SELF TEST 3

Make these conversions (each answer, 3 points).

3.01 25 cm = _____ mm

3.02 104 cm = _____ m

3.03 37 m = _____ cm

3.04 7 m = _____ mm

3.05 91 mm = _____ m

Write the metric units for these measurements (each answer, 3 points).

3.06 _____ force

3.07 _____ distance

3.08 _____ work

3.09 _____ power

3.010 _____ energy

3.011 _____ time

Write *P* for an example of potential energy, *K* for an example of kinetic energy, and *B* for an example of both (each answer, 3 points).

3.012 _____ a pigeon on a ledge

3.013 _____ a spring on a railroad bumper

3.014 _____ an airborne traffic observer

3.015 _____ a car traveling on a freeway

3.016 _____ an arrow flying in the air

Write true or false (each answer, 1 point).

3.017 _____ The energy in a compressed spring is kinetic energy.

3.018 _____ The energy of an object in motion is kinetic energy.

3.019 _____ The potential energy of an ideal pendulum at the top of its swing is equal to its kinetic energy at the bottom of its swing.

3.020 _____ If a force does not produce a change in motion, no work has been done.

3.021 _____ The energy an object possesses is equal to the work spent on the object.

3.022 _____ Galileo's concept of the sun, moon, and planets changed the prevailing thought.

3.023 _____ Newton developed a mathematical system to describe the laws of motion.

3.024 _____ The second law of motion states that a large force will produce a comparably large acceleration.

3.025 _____ The meter is a unit of measurement dating back to Biblical times.

3.026 _____ A force is a scalar quantity.

Complete these sentences (each answer, 3 points).

3.027 The ability to do work is _____ .

3.028 Energy is force times _____ .

3.029 The energy of a pendulum at the top of its swing is _____ energy.

3.030 The energy possessed by a pile driver before being released is _____ energy.

3.031 The energy of an object in motion is _____ energy.

3.032 The product of one newton of force moving an object a distance of one meter is one

_____ .

3.033 The rate at which work is done is _____ .

3.034 The Italian who observed that objects fell at the same rate was _____ .

3.035 The relationships among force, mass, and acceleration are expressed in the

_____ law of motion.

3.036 "Action-reaction" is a term commonly applied to the _____ law of motion.

Complete these activities (each answer, 5 points).

3.037 Calculate the work done when a crate weighing 13 N is carried 13 m from one loading dock to the next. _____

_____

_____

3.038 Calculate the work done on a box moved 3 meters by a force of 6 newtons.

3.039 Calculate the work done on an elevator lifted 16 feet by a force of 2500 pounds.

3.040 Find the actual distance AB from the scale drawing.

3.041 Find the vector sum of these vectors.

90 / 113   SCORE _____   TEACHER _____ _____
                                          initials   date

Before taking the LIFEPAC Test, you may want to do one or more of these self checks.

1. _____ Read the objectives. See if you can do them.
2. _____ Restudy the material related to any objectives that you cannot do.
3. _____ Use the **SQ3R** study procedure to review the material.
4. _____ Review activities, Self Tests, and LIFEPAC vocabulary words.
5. _____ Restudy areas of weakness indicated by the last Self Test.